LESSONS
FROM AN
Angel

Printed in the United States of America
Keen Vision Publishing, LLC
www.publishwithkvp.com
ISBN: 978-1-955316-97-2

LESSONS FROM AN

Angel

The Keys to Healthy Friendships

Shalicia LaShaye Torbert

In Loving Memory

ANGEL LA'VINE CONNER

(June 28, 1991 - January 18, 2020)

Table of Contents

Using your smartphone's camera, scan this code to check out a beautiful tribute video, created in loving memory of the inspiration behind this book, Angel LaVine Conner.

A BUDDY WHO BECAME OUR BABY

Our family met Angel shortly after moving from Maryland to Florida. It is hard to remember when, but at some point, she and our daughter, Shalicia (Shaye), began creating an unbreakable, life-long bond. As they began their first year of middle school, their personalities blossomed and their social circles evolved, to include more communication with each other. They lived quite a distance apart, but that obstacle was slightly alleviated when the church we all attended planted another location closer to both of our families.

At twelve, Angel appeared to be much more mature than Shaye. She had confidence that was both refreshing and scary. Once, Angel asked me, *"Why can't Shaye have her phone after 9 pm? She can always just use the house phone to call somebody."* That led to a lengthy conversation. Angel never backed down from anything she said and always just wanted to know the true answer.

Angel lived in a suburb where I taught. My students were leaps and bounds ahead in their world knowledge and understanding because they had to be! They HAD to have a level of strength and maturity to survive and thrive in their environment. I was afraid that from what I perceived that Angel may know, my daughter would be privy to things that we were determined not to expose to her yet. Little did we know, our daughter was already WAY ahead of us in her maturity level! These young ladies were on the same page and were determined to be buddies for life. Angel taught me about respect (that it works both ways between children & adults), biases (we ALL have them), and perceptions (get to know people before you make judgments). She helped me in ways that I believe she understood even more as she became an adult.

I could draft a book on the foundational aspects of her friendship with Shaye. Angel and Shaye had so many things trying to keep them apart (time, distance, school, people, and things). I would tell them that they "made me tired or sick" with what they started calling their 'shenanigans.' For an outsider to hear me say that may be negative, but they both understood what I meant. It was our language. It tickled them. I LOVED how they lived, laughed, and enjoyed their LIFE together. They traveled, argued, ate, and cooked! Whenever and wherever they could be, they were together, doing life.

Only twice did Angel ever call me to 'tell on Shaye.' She was frustrated and did not know how to resolve their disagreement. Other than that, over all those years, they fussed and argued but ALWAYS resolved their issues, with no interventions or malice. They ALWAYS landed back where they first began.

Forgiveness was another lesson they both learned from each other. They were always up to something and no matter where they were, they were going to talk every day. When they were not able to do so, it was clear. They would miss each other. Only once in a lifetime does one find a friendship like theirs. They longed to be together when they were apart, completed each other's sentences, built each other up, and promoted that which was good for the other. Until Angel left this earth in 2020, they were inseparable.

Angel loved our family and we loved her. Through the years, we saw all of her, the good, bad, and the indifferent. In turn, she saw all of us as well. It is hard to say when she became our daughter, but she did! She always supported our sons. She always supported us. She would tell my kids how smart they were, and she was such a cheerleader to us all. She deserved so much of the credit, along with Shaye and our oldest son, for helping our youngest son through the difficult years of earning his degree in mechanical engineering. Many of my tears in May 2020 (which should have been his graduation) were because she should have been there or at least on the phone. It was the height of the pandemic, but Angel would have been right with us to celebrate this milestone achievement

had she been alive.

In the span of a few short years (some back-to-back), Shaye lost her grandmother, grandfathers, godmother, cousins, aunt, great-aunts, and even a few very close friends from college. Angel was ALWAYS there or in communication. She longed to be with us for some of our family's most significant events and we treasure her for loving us as much as we loved her.

Ironically, a few of my daughter's closest friends today knew Angel. Angel spent so much time with Shaye at her college, many people thought she attended the college as well! Angel was fond of each of Shaye's close friends, and it is a 'beautiful blessing' and not a coincidence that she met them when Shaye first moved to her new city. (Casey, Tyrone, Nigel) It is almost as if she approved and ordained them to watch over Shaye when she left this earth. Each of them has played a significant role in 'looking out for Shaye' since Angel has been gone.

As an adult, Angel often texted or called my husband or me when she was having a major life experience or just to check in. She shared a special bond with my husband because he was prior military and was even her substitute teacher in high school on numerous occasions when she was in JROTC. We counted that as

an honor.

Angel could cook like a *mother*, clean like a *grandmother*, get fine like an *auntie*, and slay your face like a *cousin*! She was a fantastic make-up artist. Angel was one of the most talented, intelligent, and brilliant people that I have ever known. Angel could get a good job so easily. It is remarkable how resilient and unstoppable she was. I never missed an opportunity to tell her how proud she made me.

Though she was very fun and kind, Angel was private. She did not fool with everybody, yet so many saw her as one of their closest friends. This is a testament to the type of person she was. She could make you feel like you were the only one that mattered. I think that is a HUGE quality that comes directly from God. She made people feel special, relevant, and seen, even while she experienced so many personal hardships and struggles. No matter what obstacles she faced, she persevered and pressed forward.

We were so proud of her when she first joined the Army. As a teenager, she had once asked me about the Army, when she was planning to join ROTC. She was so serious as we discussed what it was like to be a Black woman in the military. She was very young at the time, but that is just how reflective and brilliant Angel was.

It has been said and it is ever so true, that she was named by her parents accordingly and with such purpose. It certainly was not the purpose any of us planned or could ever imagine. However, I KNOW that we were so blessed to have this young woman in our lives. We will continue to uphold, support, share, and remember her integrity, military service, and legacy with her family and her son. We will never forget her. During her homegoing service and as they fought for her justice, her parents generously acknowledged us as her godparents. It is an honor that we do not take it lightly. We will forever be grateful that they understood what she meant to us and we to her.

Angel touched so many lives. Stories are still being told about her generosity, wisdom, courage, strength, beauty, and most of all, her friendship. No matter where we go and how many years pass, we can all be assured that we were indeed touched, in this life, by OUR ANGEL!

True friendship is hard to find, build, and keep, but when you do, your life will be all the more fulfilling. As you read this book, compiled by our daughter, Shaye, we hope you will reflect on the beauty of friendship. May this book lead you to recognize and value the angels God sends your way in the form of friends.

-Shelton & Yvette Torbert

Introduction

THE TRUE MEANING OF FRIENDSHIP

Angel La'Vine Conner was very instrumental in helping me become the woman I am today. I cannot imagine the person I would be without the impact Angel had on my life as my best friend. We shared a bond many people might not ever get to experience in their lifetime, and I am honored God blessed me with my very own Angel on Earth. We had so much fun every time we were together. Angel taught me how to enjoy every day and cherish every opportunity as if it were my last. Angel and I always knew we had something special, but we never understood the magnitude of what we shared. More than anything, our experiences taught me a lot about the true meaning of friendship.

Friday, January 17th, 2020, I took my friend's daughter, whom I like to call my Hannah Banana, to Disney World's Magic Kingdom in Orlando, Florida.

I was chosen to represent my organization at Walt Disney World's Leadership Institute. After our training courses and leadership activities were up for the week, they provided us with tickets to visit all of the theme parks. So that Friday and Saturday, Hannah and I planned to do the 15 safari tours at Animal Kingdom, see the animals, and ride all the rides. On Friday, we rode Space Mountain and fought through a lot of people to get front-row seats to see the fireworks display over Cinderella's castle. We took pictures, sent them to Angel, and she loved them! I video-called

Angel before we left for Disney, and she told me that she was headed out. On our way home, I called her again to see if she was back home and she told me that she was still out and enjoying herself as well. I could hear music and people in the background. It sounded like Angel was having a good time. I couldn't wait to hear all about it, so I told her to text me when she got home. She texted me when she got home around 1 am, Saturday morning, January 18th and we gossiped back and forth about our night. The conversation was so good, I ended up telling her a secret, and she promised to take it to her grave. I know she kept that promise because a few short hours later, she was taken from us forever.

"Hey, friend! I'm so lit right now!"

I keep hearing her sounding so excited and full of life in my head. I could have never guessed that would be the last time I heard her voice.

After our last text, early Saturday morning, Angel was brutally murdered in her own home during a domestic violence dispute. She was shot six times by a man, a coward, who claimed he loved and cared for her. I do not think it coincidental that I was in Florida at the exact time, even though I resided in Washington, D.C. God placed me there specifically to be with her family during that life changing moment. I was able to be there for them in their darkest hour as they received the terrible news. Although her story has touched and reached many people in her death, I want people to know the Angel that I knew while she was alive.

Angel was an exemplary role model for everything a friend should be. The lessons she taught me about being a true friend are lessons that I will carry with me for the rest of my life. I was very angry when Angel left me, but as I began to remember her for who she was and not the way she was taken from us, I realized she left me with a gift to share with the world.

In addition to being a memorial to the life and legacy of Angel, this book is also a guide to help you become a better friend and develop stronger friendships. Many people use the words friend or best friend very loosely. Most don't know how to be a good friend.

There are many characteristics that a true friend will display, and in this book, I share the lessons I learned from my Angel on choosing friends and what qualities one must possess to be a good friend. Losing Angel taught me how powerful it is to have solid friendships, but grieving her death opened my eyes to the beautiful friendships I had all around me. Angel was such a gift to this world, and as you read this book, I hope you receive the gift of understanding true friendship.

What About Your Friends?

Insert a picture of you and your best friend(s)!

"One who has unreliable friends soon comes to ruin, but there is a friend who sticks closer than a brother."

Proverbs 18:24 (NLT)

In this picture, Angel and I were in middle school. It was the beginning of our friendship, and we had no clue how our bond would blossom into something unimaginable. Although we never went to the same school or lived in the same city, we were inseparable. This distance never mattered. If Angel and I weren't physically together, we were together in spirit. We were so connected, I could feel her thinking about me. I knew when my phone was about to ring and could pick up on her feelings whenever we talked. Nine times out of ten, if you talked to either of us separately, on any given day, we could tell you what the other had for breakfast or dinner. We talked that much. She was the sister I never had. She was closer to me than my sister probably would have been. That bond came from years of getting to know Angel, understanding her personality, and learning her story.

When I think of a friend that sticks closer than a brother, I imagine a best friend. Someone closer to you than your blood should most definitely hold the title of best friend in your heart. Those friends are always a blessing to have around. The closeness

Proverbs 18:24 refers to isn't physical. You don't have to be stuck to a person's side day in and day out to be close. It's about being close in mind, spirit, and soul. The bond of true best friends is hard to come by, and even harder to keep. However, when you are committed to learning and growing with your best friend, the love you share can transcend any bump or obstacle in the road.

"Compromise is what binds people together. Compromise is sharing and conciliatory; it is loving and kind and unselfish."

Ali Harris, The First Last Kiss

Angel and I rarely had to compromise because we often wanted the same things. Angel loved Moe's and I love Chipotle, but at times, we both sacrificed our preferences to make the other happy. We never saw it as a hassle. We knew that to keep our bond healthy, we had to compromise and meet in the middle.

One year, we went to Miami for Memorial Day weekend. I really wanted to attend the Young Jeezy Concert, but Angel wanted to see if we could find cheaper tickets. We never did, so we ended up at a different club looking at August Alsina. She happened to be a fan, but I wasn't. The truth of the matter is, we could have gone to either concert and had a blast simply because we were together.

The picture above captures an element I believe every friendship should possess. You see, it appears that Angel and I are the same height. When in reality, she was much taller than me. I gave a little by standing on my tiptoes, and she took a little by crouching down. We did what we needed to do to be on the same page. That's what real friends do. The give and take aspect of any relationship can be tedious. However, it is necessary to ensure relationships are mutually beneficial. It's not about keeping score or remembering who gave the last time. True friends do what needs to be done in every circumstance to ensure they are on the same page. Placing someone else's desires or needs before your own is a selfless skill that few people possess. Compromise can be hard, but it is the lifeblood of long-lasting friendships.

"Don't make friends who are comfortable to be with. Make friends who will force you to level up."

Thomas J. Watson

S ome people only want the best for you if what's best suits them. If what's best for you takes you on a different path, many won't encourage you to move forward. Real friends, however, are different. They want what's best for you unconditionally. It doesn't matter if it's comfortable or acceptable to them. They want you to be the person you were created to be with or without them. Real friends keep this same energy even if your needs don't benefit them.

As kids, Angel and I were always up to something. We had each others' backs no matter what. When faced with situations that could have had major consequences, Angel would always tell me, *"You are going to be someone great someday. Don't do that!"* I would always reply, *"Well, if you are going to do it, then I am too!"* I was adamant about letting her know that I was with her in everything, even if it had nothing to do with me. She, on the other hand, could often see more in me than I saw in myself. As a result, she did her best to help me keep my future at the forefront of my mind.

A good off-guard picture can tell a beautiful story, and this picture is no different. We were in Las Vegas, and Angel captured this picture while I wasn't looking. When we got home, she sent me the picture and said, *"I want you to see what I see! You look so pretty!"* This picture always reminds me of the solidity of our bond. In this day and age, everyone is out for themselves, seeking what they can gain from every connection. If you have friends who see the best in you, push you to be better, and always remind you of your awesomeness, love them well! They are indeed a rarity.

FRIENDS THAT STAY READY

So, if you stay ready, you don't have to get ready; and that is how I run my life.

Will Smith

We would always say, *"When you stay ready you don't have to get ready!"* Well, as you can see, Angel was still getting ready when the camera flashed! We were about to ride the "Slotzilla" zipline in Vegas, and of course, took advantage of the opportunity to take a picture. We loved taking pictures! Before it was our turn, we witnessed how quickly they snapped everyone's photo, giving them no time to get situated. I assumed Angel was preparing before it was our turn. Of course, being the diva that she was, Angel had to check her outfit for the fifth time. They took the picture as she was looking down, and there were no do-overs! Nevertheless, I still love this picture of us because at least one of us was ready!

Ready friends are more than just picture-ready. Friends who stay ready are always prepared to have your back, speak up for you, and be there for you. They don't have to think before they defend you in a room full of your enemies. They don't have to think before jumping into action when you are in need. These types of friends are there for you, and ready to ride before you finish sharing the problem. Don't get me wrong, staying ready for your friends is not about self-neglect or being available at the drop of a dime. Realistically, this is impossible as life can be a lot, especially as adults. Rather, the idea of staying ready is about your heart posture as a friend. When you truly love and care for your friend, you don't have to question if or how you should be there during their time of need. Real friends just show up.

Though in this picture, Angel was NOT ready, I am grateful to have experienced a loving friend who was always ready to be there for me.

What About Your Friends?

Insert a picture of you and your best friend(s)
in your best "stay ready" poses!

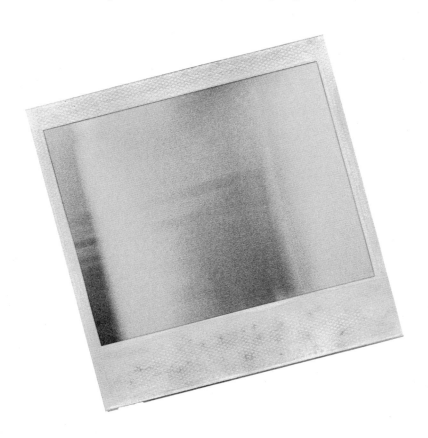

FRIENDS THAT DON'T HIDE
HOW THEY FEEL

*"Being honest may not get you a lot
of friends but it'll always get you
the right ones."*

John Lennon

It never failed. On every trip, Angel and I would run ourselves into the ground, not pausing a moment for sleep. No matter how tired we were, the party must go on! The night we took this photo was no different. We were in Las Vegas and had overbooked ourselves. We spent all day at pool parties and had tickets for a Michael Jackson show that evening. Before we left our hotel for the show, Angel said, *"I'm tired."* I immediately caught an attitude. I rolled my eyes and said, *"We can miss the show if you're so tired."* She dismissed me and went to get ready. The truth is, I was tired too, but I didn't want our shenanigans to stop. Hearing my friend stand in her truth made me want to own mine as well. *"Actually, I'm tired too!"* I told her. She just laughed. We talked about our busy day and acknowledged that we were tired. However, because we both knew the show must go on, we sucked it up, got some 5-hour energy shots, and had one of the best nights of our life!

You need friends who aren't afraid to be honest, even if their feelings differ from yours. Sometimes, their honesty can be as simple as admitting that they are tired, or as heavy as admitting that they feel lost in their lives. Healthy friendships should always have an open-door policy for honesty. A little honesty can go a long way. It's hard to build a lasting friendship when two individuals are dishonest about what they feel. Honesty opens the stage for true bonds to develop. When friends feel like they can be honest with each other, they don't run away from the friendship when things go wrong. Instead, they will run to the safety the relationship provides.

Be honest with your friends, and allow them the space to be honest with you. Who knows? You both may be feeling the same way and can help each other press through!

FRIENDS THAT UNDERSTAND
WHAT YOU'VE BEEN THROUGH

*"A friend understands your past,
believes in your future, and accepts
you just the way you are."*

Unknown

It's hard to bond with anyone if you don't understand their past and the circumstances that made them who they are. Let's say your friend gets outrageously upset when someone cancels plans with them. If you knew that when they were younger, their parent would cancel plans to see them every weekend, you would understand why they had trust issues. Those who are privileged to call you their friend must have an understanding of your makeup and the reasons behind your behavior. This requires honesty and vulnerability, but it's worth it. When you are triggered or experience difficulty, it's easy to be there for each other when you have a deeper understanding of one another.

One Sunday, after church, Angel and I decided to grab lunch. Going out to eat after church was always our tradition, but this Sunday, my friend Brittany joined us. When the bill came, Brittany paid for my food. I started to cry. No one my age had ever done such a thing for me. I was accustomed to taking care of and being a blessing to others. That day, God reminded me that I wasn't forgotten. Brittany was like, *"It's just food. It's okay."*

Angel spoke up for me, *"No one has ever done that for Shaye. That's why she is emotional."*

From the moment our bond formed, Angel had been there to explain why I felt the way I did. She took the time to understand my life, what I had been through, and why I behaved the way I did. She was the one friend who really knew why I became the woman I am today. Our friendship was far from perfect, but because we understood each other, it was easy to maneuver through the challenges and obstacles that came our way. Our understanding of each other ensured that we fought fair and attacked the issue rather than each other.

Tell your friends what you have gone through, and listen as they share their story. It will make a world of a difference in your friendships.

*"I would rather walk with a friend
in the dark, than alone in the light."*
Helen Keller

Do you desire to make new friends? Have you ever seen a group of friends hanging out, having a blast, and wished you could have that experience? To make friends, you must be willing to show yourself friendly. Sometimes, we are afraid to simply smile or start a light conversation with others. We allow ourselves to overthink it, or second-guess our ability to be interesting enough to talk with strangers. When we show ourselves as friendly to others, we allow ourselves the opportunity to make new connections. After all, we were created to connect with others. As human beings, it is impossible to survive without other humans. Why not make a few friends along our journey?

Angel had so many friends because she was friendly. She was always positive, wore a beautiful smile, and had a welcoming attitude toward anyone she met. Now, if you were to cross her, you would have had a different encounter!

When I first saw Angel, she looked so mature that I thought she was much older than me. She sat with her older sister at Bible Study, and always wore big gold hoops and a gold necklace. One day, she smiled at me, I smiled back, and we started a conversation. *"I thought you were in high school!"* I shared when she told me her age.

"I thought you were older than me too!" She said in her angelic voice. After a smile and a kind chat, we realized we were the same age and began what would one day become the most beautiful friendship I would ever know. I can't imagine having missed the opportunity to create a bond with her because I was too shy to smile or say hello. We both showed ourselves friendly and built a friendship I will tell my kids and her son about when they are older.

A simple hello, or a kind smile can be the difference between making a new friend or being dissatisfied that you don't have the friendships that you desire. Show yourself friendly! There are people out there waiting to connect with you.

A Tribute to Our Angel

A FRIEND WHO BELIEVED IN ME

TARA COOPER

I met Angel while I was in AIT for the Army at Fort Leonard Wood, MO. Being away from home, the military has a way of connecting people, and ironically, Conner and I bonded because we were both from Florida. I knew we would grow to have a friendship, but I never imagined how close we would become. We talked about everything, she listened, advised, and never judged me. Some people come into your life for a reason and some for a season, but Angel definitely came into my life to serve a purpose. I wish that words could express the impression she made on my life in such a short time, but the feeling is unforgettable. Not only did I see that she cared, but I felt it and that's rare in a friendship. Even in basic training, she would defend my stuttering when other people made fun of me. She would get mad

before I could even respond to them. I will forever be grateful that I experienced the genuine love Angel gave to those she cared about. Our talks will forever replay in my mind. I will forever be grateful to God for a friendship like ours and the time we were able to spend together.

Angel
and
Friends

FRIENDS THAT ARE
READY FOR ADVENTURE

"We didn't even realize we were making memories. We just knew we were having fun."

Winnie the Pooh

A dventures are unusual, exciting, typically hazardous, once-in-a-lifetime experiences or activities. You don't know what to expect, how to prepare, or how the experience will end. Most time, you don't even know that it's on the way, and that's the beauty of it all. Adventures make life more meaningful, especially when with friends. There is nothing more exciting than gearing up for an adventure with your friends, and spending hours laughing and talking about it later. Adventures are opportunities to create memories for a lifetime. Friends that enjoy adventures together bond on a deeper level. If you are looking for a way to deepen your friendships, or switch up your brunch routine, go on an adventure with your friends!

In this picture, Angel and I were on one of our many adventures. When we left the hotel, we didn't know we were getting on a roller coaster. We were walking to CVS to get Tylenol for our 'fun vegas night' hangovers, heard the roller coaster, and decided to get on it. Neither of us wanted to take the picture because we looked like a hot mess, but we decided we needed it for memories and scrapbooking purposes. Sometimes in life, we wake up expecting one thing, and the next thing we know, we are on a roller coaster. Choose friends that are willing to ride with you no matter how you look or how much you scream through it. A good friend will hold your hand, scream with you, and be there with you until the end of the ride.

TAMPA

FRIENDS THAT AREN'T HATERS

"When people don't want the best for you, they are not the best for you."

Gayle King

Friendships consist of two or more individuals on different paths that chose to journey together. Naturally, there will be seasons when one friend is in a better position financially, educationally, emotionally, relationally, physically, etc. However, in true friendships, the difference in seasons never causes hate or envy in the bond. In authentic friendships, one friend can be healing from heartbreak but still genuinely celebrate the other friend's new boo. A real friend will rejoice with you about your new promotion, even as they are on the job hunt for themselves. You may be going through a rough time with your family, but you can still see the beauty in your friends' bond with their families. Real friends support each other through every accomplishment, failure, high, and low.

Angel was there for each of my accomplishments and was genuinely happy for me. I did the same for her. In this photo, we were enjoying my last day in Tampa before my job moved me to Washington, D.C. I was extremely happy to have my best friend with me as I prepared to embark upon a new adventure. Angel supported me as I bid farewell to college life and ventured into adulthood. We couldn't wait for me to get settled in D.C. so she could visit. Many people expressed they wanted to see me before I left, but my best friend was one of the few who came through for me. I didn't expect anything less. We always showed up for each other.

There was never jealousy between us. We were always overjoyed for each other, no matter the accomplishment. We felt each other's wins and losses. If I had it, she had it. If she had it, I had it. Her accomplishments were my accomplishments. My accomplishments were her accomplishments. That was the way things went for me and Angel.

As you reflect on your friendships, ask yourself the following questions.

- Am I envious of my friends' achievements? If so, why?
- How do my friends show their support?
- How do I show up for my friends?

FRIENDS THAT ENCOURAGE
YOUR CONFIDENCE

"Go, best friend! We killing 'em!"
Coi Leray

One thing about a best friend is that they will boost your self-confidence. On your worst days when you are feeling your worst, real friends will swoop in, remind you who you are, and force you to get up, get dressed, and flaunt your smile! Friends let you know that you look amazing before you head out. Preparing for a big test or event? Good friends will encourage you every step of the way and constantly remind you: *"You've got this!"* Friends should always push each other to feel their best!

Everyone in this picture, besides Angel and I, were teenagers on spring break from college. This 'photo shoot' began after we all watched Angel strike a few poses on the stairs. As I snapped photos of her, I saw how they admired her confidence. So I said, *"Hey! Do y'all want to take a picture too?"* Their confidence was still loading, but Angel made everyone in this picture feel like they were somebody! Confidence is contagious, and Angel brought out confidence in everyone around her.

Do you bring out the best in your friends? Do they bring out the best in you? Having healthy and supportive friends automatically increases your confidence. Knowing that you have good friends in your corner gives you the confidence to step out into the world and own it!

What About Your Friends?

Insert a picture of you and your best friend(s)
looking and feeling confident!

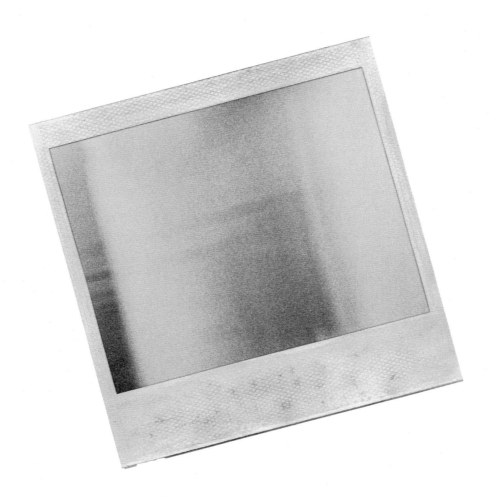

"I've seen you at your worst and I still think you're the best."

Unknown

T ake a moment and think back to your 'pre-glow-up' days. The days you thought you were hot stuff, but when you look at pictures you wonder, *"What on Earth was I wearing? Why does my hair look like that? What's up with my eyebrows? Who let me purchase those shoes?!"* Oh, and make no mistake about it. It wasn't just your attire in need of some adjustments. Can you remember the decisions you made back then? The way you reacted to trivial matters? Your attitude towards life? The pre-glow-up times are cringeworthy for everyone!

While your mind is still reminiscing, take a moment and think about the friends that surrounded you during that time. Though you all were probably in the process of glowing up, it's always easier to see the flaws of others than your own. Your friends probably saw the areas of your life that needed a little revamping. If they were good friends, they probably even talked to you about it. Friends who stick beside you before the glow-up are one in a million. It's not hard to make and keep friends when you have it all together. However, genuine friends are placed in our lives to walk with us as we glow up! In this photo, Angel and I were headed to our Pastor's 50th Birthday Party. My mom bought me two dresses to choose from. Angel happened to sleep over the night before, so we both wore one. Angel chose the long dress with the v-cut. I was so happy because I was afraid to rock that much cleavage. Also, Angel was taller than me, so the dress fit her perfectly. We couldn't wait to get to the party. We thought were the finest little women in the room. Boy, were we wrong!

Though we both HATE this picture, it's proof that Angel and I walked with each other through our glow-up — physically, mentally, and emotionally. The truth is, we should never stop glowing up. It is important to have genuine friends who will walk with you every step of the way!

What About Your Friends?

Insert a throwback picture of you and your best friend(s)!

"We have been friends together... in sunshine and in shade. "

Caroline Norton

Would you check out this glow-up? Almost eight years later, Angel and I attended another pastor's anniversary in Huntsville, AL, where Rickey Smiley was the guest entertainer. Angel didn't have a ticket to attend the show, but that didn't stop her from making that 10-hour drive. The cool thing is, she ended up managing my brother's artwork table with other vendors during the show and still got to meet Rickey Smiley behind the scenes! That totally made her night! And, to think, this trip almost didn't happen! Angel was fashionably late and I almost left without her. But, how could I leave my bestie behind? Never in a million years!

It's sad to say, but everyone can't handle your glow-up! Some will feel like you've changed and switched up. Make sure that those you call friends aren't offended by your glow-up. Also, make sure that as a friend, you aren't envious of the glow-up happening around you. We are all constantly growing, changing, and maturing! That process alone can be daunting. Good friends who root for us along the way make the process even sweeter.

Selfless means being more concerned with the needs and wishes of others than one's own. In this day and age, everyone is out for themselves, and their agenda. It's no wonder why friendships don't last as long as they did back in the day. There are people in older generations that have been friends for decades, through trial, circumstance, disagreement, frustration, heartbreak, and more. This generation struggles to understand how to balance being selfless and caring for self.

Very often in friendships, there will be times when all individuals must practice selflessness to be there for each other in good times, and in bad times. We cannot become so consumed with personal life circumstances that we miss the opportunity to be there for others.

As we matured, Angel and I learned more and more about what it means to be selfless in our friendship. This photo means so much to me for many reasons. In May 2013, I graduated from college. Angel was stationed in El Paso, Texas and she had just given birth to Stephon A'marri Butler. Though I had not seen her in two years and missed her dearly, I knew that there was no way she was going to make it to my graduation in Tampa FL. She couldn't take leave because she had just had a baby. The week leading up to my graduation, her relationship, at the time, took a drastic turn. Fortunately, she was able to escape with her life and her child, and she moved back to Florida immediately. I was excited that she was back in Florida, but didn't dare put pressure on her to attend my graduation.

We texted and called each other all day. I may have been texting her while I was waiting on my name to be called at graduation! I sent her a picture of me in my cap and gown. She told me how proud she was of me and that she knew I could do it! I always loved how proud she was of me.

After graduation, my parents planned a celebration brunch at one of the local hotels. And guess who walked in, fashionably late per usual: My Angel! I was overjoyed. She had tried to make the graduation ceremony but got lost. She was there for one of the biggest days of my life despite what she was going through. I never forgot that moment.

Life is filled with difficulties. Sometimes, showing up for our friends allows us to escape from it all. Seeing their smiling faces warms our hearts and encourages us to keep pressing forward. A little selflessness goes a long way for everyone involved. Challenge yourself to be more selfless in your friendships!

Key 14

FRIENDS THAT ARE SURVIVORS

*"I'm a survivor! I'm gonna make it!
I will survive! Keep on survivin'!"*
Destiny's Child, Survivor

One of the things I admired most about Angel is that she was a survivor. Through the years, I watched my friend face many difficulties. Through everything she experienced, she stayed true to herself, and made the most of her situation. She inspired me to look at my life challenges through a different lens. Her strength, just like everything else about her, was contagious. I wanted to be stronger because Angel was strong. I admired her tenacity so much.

In this picture, I am hugging her son, and thanking him for bringing his mom back home to us safely. You see, Stephon saved her life. If it wasn't for Angel wanting him to grow up in a household filled with love, she would have never left the relationship she was in. She always wanted what was best for Stephon. There was nothing she wouldn't do to make sure he had the best life possible, even if it meant buying a one-way ticket home, becoming a reservist in the military, and working three jobs. She did whatever needed to be done for her son. Do you have any friends who are survivors? Take every chance you get to let them know how much you admire their strength and courage!

Angel
and
Stephon

"How we smart enough to make these millions...Strong enough to bear the children...Then get back to business."
Run the World (Girls), Beyoncé

As we journey into adulthood, we take on many hats. We become parents, spouses, leaders in our careers, and so much more. Many times, roles we had previously take a backseat as we learn how to wear our new hats. More than likely, our friendships take huge hits that can be hard to recover from. The key is learning how to wear all hats well! This is easier said than done, but it helps when you have friends who are understanding and everyone does their best to keep the lines of communication open.

Angel and I were definitely feeling ourselves in this picture. We were out celebrating my graduation, and this was her first night out since she had Stephon. All night long, she complained about her feet hurting and missing her baby! I chuckled to myself every time. I was so amazed by my friend. How she balanced being a mother, friend, and so much more blew my mind. During this time, her dad had also been having health troubles. She spent many nights at the hospital to comfort him and her family and be their backbone in tough times.

If you or your friends are learning how to juggle multiple major responsibilities, it's important to be kind and understanding to one another. Even if you have different responsibilities, there is so much you can learn from watching each other navigate. Also, be sure to look for opportunities to encourage and support each other. Whether it's a listening ear or lending a helping hand, there is always a way to be there for each other, regardless of how busy you both may be.

"A jealous close friend is more dangerous than a friendly hidden enemy."

Unknown

real friend should never be envious of your dealings with other people. If they are truly your friend, they will recognize that they are not the only person who is attracted to the great person you are. I have a very extensive network, and I have friends from all different walks of life. Angel was never jealous of my other friends. There were times in my life when I had too many people around me and Angel could point out who wasn't a real friend and who was just along for the ride. I made sure Angel knew her place in my life when it came to those individuals and we both acted accordingly. It was also important to me that everyone knew who my best friend was. She knew her place in my life, so there was never any confusion about other friends. When Angel met any of my other friends they already knew who she was because I always talked about her, and she already knew who they were because I talked to her about everything.

When Angel met my dear friend Casey, she loved how sweet she was and immediately recognized what a good friend she was to me. There was never any battle about who was the better friend.

Everyone knew their place in my life. Even though Casey and I had only been friends for about a year, Angel could see that her intentions for me were just as good as someone who had known me my whole life. One day while we were in Cleveland, Ohio celebrating my 27th birthday, Angel told Casey, "You are so sweet. You are exactly the friend that I want to take care of Shaye when I'm not here." Thinking back on that comment, Angel was referring to the fact that she would be far away in Oklahoma, but her words resonated with us because now they mean so much more. Angel recognized that I needed other good friends in my life and because she didn't mind sharing me with other people, those people were there to comfort me as I dealt with the loss of her.

The key to balancing friends is to make sure everyone feels important, and no one feels slighted. Friendships always flow smoother when everyone is clear on their role in each other's lives.

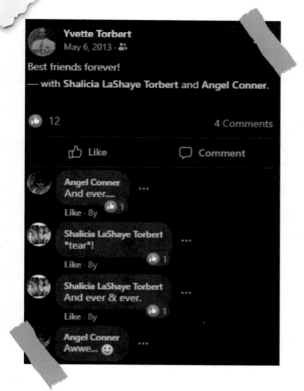

Key 17

FRIENDS THAT ARE THERE THROUGH THICK AND THIN

"Anyone can show up when you're happy. But the ones who stay by yourside when your heart falls apart, they are your true friends."

Brigitte Nicole

O ne day, Angel's mother asked her if we ever argued, and Angel's response was, *"YES! We argue!"* We did argue and if we weren't arguing, there was sure to be a disagreement somewhere because we believed two different ways about a subject.

No one really ever knew because we kept our arguments to ourselves. The few times our parents did know we were arguing, they looked the other way because they knew we would work through it. One time, we had a big disagreement when we were in Miami and didn't talk for almost a week after we got back. It was treacherous, to say the least. Even if we thought we weren't going to be friends after that, no one had the idea to run and spread each other's business or bad mouth each other to someone else.

One thing I have seen friends do after breakups is run and tell all of their business. That is not what a real friend does. Even if you are not friends anymore, you held that sacred spot once in a person's life and they trusted you with their information at the time. Angel and I would always promise to take each other's secrets to the grave! She took my secrets with her and I will honor her and do the same. Just like every relationship, friendships go through ups and downs. No one agrees all the time. Disagreements are a natural interaction between two individuals. What matters is how you disagree! The actions you take and the things you say during a disagreement can have a lasting impact on any relationship. Just because you disagree doesn't mean you should throw away the bond. Some disagreements do not constitute the end of the friendship. If we all disconnected from each other because of disagreements, no one would be friends! Healthy, long-lasting friendships require the ability to withstand challenging moments. Make sure you select friends who are willing to rise above petty arguments and disagreements to still see value in the friendship!

A Tribute to Our Angel

A HOSPITABLE FRIEND

SPC ANNIE WILLIAMS

Angel was one of the most hospitable people I knew. She was always willing to open her home and provide a place of comfort for anyone. I remember reporting back to work after maternity leave, and Angel was working in the section I was assigned to. One day, I walked in with my lunch bag and she asked, *"What did you cook?"* I answered, *"Just some chicken and veggies."* She said, *"It smells so good. What did you put on it?"* I said, *"Just some lemon pepper and a little bacon grease on the veggies."* She said, "Oh girl, I know you can cook!" That following weekend we had tacos at my house.

We all knew SPC Conner loved to cook and she didn't mind sharing what she cooked. On her last Thanksgiving, she hosted a good number of soldiers in her home and cooked a Thanksgiving meal that many of them will never forget. She prepared it with the energy and love that we don't see too often in young people. It was as if her grandmother was cooking through her.

I truly believed she knew just how loved she was. Angel was kind, charismatic, and gentle. Her beauty shined inside and out. She worked hard at everything she put her hands on, and no task was impossible. She touched so many in various ways. Where some of us saw problems, Angel saw opportunities. I am grateful for having the chance to meet her and become more than just a co-worker, but a friend. We would always get in trouble because our 1SG would find us together giggling and laughing! Our trips to the Shoppette, simply eating lunch together or doing what we do best…working, I'll never forget! She was an outstanding soldier, a loving mother, a caring friend, an amazing sibling, and an incredible daughter. I miss my dear Angel. She left us beautiful memories, and her love is still my guide. Though I cannot see her, she's always at my side.

"Friendships should be built on a solid foundation of alchohol, sarcasm, inappropriateness, and shenanigans."
Unknown

Angel and I never knew what to expect when we went anywhere, but we knew we would have fun! Thus, shenanigans became our favorite term to sum up what it was like when we were together. We had the best times ever! Whether we were bowling, walking in the park, on the strip in Vegas, or walking in the grocery store. Everything was an adventure for us. Now, as I go through life, I make the best of every experience. If I am not having fun, I do something to make it fun! Whether I have to take a drink or do something crazy, I am determined to make memories that will last a lifetime.

We often think that in order to have a good time, we have to do something elaborate or expensive. However, with fun friends, doing anything can become memorable! Things like sleepovers or small house parties can be a blast. It's a lot easier to have fun with friends who enjoy living life to the fullest. These people will make the most of any moment, and challenge you to do the same. If you surround yourself with others who strive to see the beauty in life, your time together will be full of memories that you'll never forget.

What About Your Friends?

Insert pictures of your favorite shenanigans with friends!

"Remember, George, no man is a failure who has friends."

It's A Wonderful Life

"N*o one is more professional than I. I am a noncommissioned officer, a leader of Soldiers.*" This is a quote from the Army's NCO Creed. I am not in the military but I cannot get that line out of my head thanks to Angel.

Angel was determined to succeed and become an NCO once she got back on active duty in the Army, and I was determined to help my friend accomplish her goals. To help her memorize the Creed, she sent it to me and recited it every morning when we talked. I felt like by the time she finished learning it, I would need to take my talents to the military as well for I would know the whole NCO Creed too!

To get back on active duty, she had to change her diet. She ate healthy to make the weight requirement to get back in the military, so I ate healthy too. If she had a salad, I ate a salad. If she was fasting, I was fasting. It was funny because we loved to eat, but I refused to tempt her or worsen her struggle to get back in the military.

One night when we lived together, we went to bed hungry, and I joked, *"Let's drink two bottles of water and have sleep for dinner!"* We laughed and went to bed, only to be awakened by growling stomachs in the midnight hour. We were up at three a.m., frying eggs because that was the lightest thing we could think to eat that was still good. I wanted to see my friend meet her goals, get back into the military, and succeed at the highest level possible.

FRIENDS THAT CHOOSE YOU

"You got troubles, I've got 'em too. There isn't anything I wouldn't do for you. We stick together and see it through. 'Cause you've got a friend in me."

You've Got A Friend in Me,
Toy Story

In many ways, a real friendship is a lot like marriage. At least our friendship was. We were there for better or for worse, rich or poor, and through sickness and health. There were many times we got mad at each other. Angel was moody and I was mean at times. In the end, she always chose me and I always chose her. We both had our faults but we never let them take over our friendship. We would stay mad for fifteen minutes then be back together. Friends do argue, and even fall out but the way you handle situations when you are angry shows how strong your friendship is.

The key is remembering to fight the problem and not each other. Many times, we are frustrated with the issue, but take it out on each other. Healthy conflict is good for friendships because it allows you both to become stronger in problem-solving together. No matter the challenge you face, choose each other and the friendship over the situation. Problems come and go, but solid friends are hard to come by. Treasure them while you can, and protect the bond from trivial matters that won't matter five years from now!

Angel
and
Friends

FRIENDS THAT CHEER YOU ON

"Oh, I get by with a little help from my friends. Mm, gonna try with a little help from my friends."
With a Little Help From My Friends,
The Beatles

Angel was always rooting for me. If I thought I did badly on a test in school she would say, *"Girl! I know you passed it!"* If I ever thought I wouldn't do well on something or get a position, she was always there to root me on. The first time I vividly remember her encouragement was in 8th grade when Angel and I were just beginning our friendship. One day, my mom took us to see the SpongeBob SquarePants Movie. Angel was decked out in Spongebob gear from head to toe. She had on a SpongeBob shirt, jean shorts, knee-high SpongeBob socks, and a matching yellow and blue SpongeBob backpack. She loved SpongeBob! The day before, I attended cheerleading tryouts for my middle school cheerleading squad and the results would be posted during the time we were at the movies. Since I had plans, I asked a friend to call me with the results.

Well, my friend called me on the way to the movies to inform me that I didn't make the team. I cried all the way to the movie theater. My mom asked if I wanted to go see the list for myself, and I said, *"No."* I was just devastated. Angel encouraged me to go look for myself. I can still hear her voice now, *"You should go look for yourself, Shaye!"* After a lot of encouragement, Angel and my mom finally convinced me to go to the school and see the list before we went into the movie.

When we pulled up to the school, I got out and walked over to the front doors to look at the pitiful list. As I scanned the list, I thought to myself your last name starts with a 't', so look at the bottom! The last name on the list was 'Shalicia Torbert.' I screamed back to my mom and Angel, *"MY NAME IS ON THE LIST!!!"* The girl only knew me as 'Shaye' not Shalicia, that's why she told me I didn't make the team. When I got back in the truck all I can hear is Angel saying, *"See, Shaye! I told you! I told you would make the team!"*

Just like your mail man needs a mail man, this cheerleader needed her own cheerleader! Angel and my mom cheered me on and boosted my confidence in my ability to make the team!

Key 22

FRIENDS THAT STICK UP FOR YOU

"Strong people stand up for themselves, but stronger people stand up for others."

Unknown

F riends should always have each other's back, publicly and privately. Having your friend's back isn't just lip service. Your actions should always line up with what you say. Angel always had my back. Looking back, I think she had my back more than I had hers. One time, we attended a college football game with another friend of mine and ended up sitting behind some drunk frat boys. One of the frat boys spilled a drink on my friend and I started arguing with him. Before the argument got too heated, I walked away because I didn't want things to escalate and get kicked out of the game. I wanted to stay at the football game to watch someone play who probably wasn't even checking for me.

When I came back, the frat boy picked up where we left off. Anyone who knows Angel knows she is not the one to stand by and watch someone get bullied. Before he could even get too close to my face, he was on the ground and security was escorting Angel out. I was so mad at Angel for escalating the situation, but her response was, *"He was going to hit you! I wasn't going to let that happen."* After they escorted Angel out, I stayed behind with the friend Angel had defended on my behalf. That day, I was not a good friend to Angel. I should have left with her. Other factors influenced my decision to stay at the time, but the fact remains that she had my back so I should have had hers. Even though she shouldn't have escalated the problem, I should have left with her and told her how I felt when we got home. That is what friends do for each other. If you are ever fortunate enough to have a friend who will stick up for you, come hell or high water, you should be there to do the same for them.

FRIENDS THAT TAKE CHANCES

"What do you say to taking chances?
What do you say to jumping off the
edge?"

Taking Chances, Celine Dion

hat is life if we never take chances? If we only do comfortable things, what memories will we have to reflect on when we get older? Taking chances can be risky, but that's the entire point of it all! If we never push our limits, we never know how far we can really go. Though we may not know the outcome, we come out on the other side with more confidence and assurance that no matter what life throws our way, we have what it takes to face it head-on. Taking chances is even more rewarding when you do it with friends that have the same mindset. Doing things that get your adrenaline pumping with friends allows you to bond, make memories, and develop a deeper trust in each other.

Angel and I took a lot of chances together and individually. In this picture, we are in Las Vegas on a zipline that was 51 stories high. The ride would whisk us between two buildings at 35mph, with nothing but pavement and people enjoying their vacation below. Angel and I both had a fear of heights, but we held hands and encouraged each other not to look down. We were terrified, and prayed that the seats would hold us! We survived and had a blast. The thrill of doing it together on vacation made it so much better.

In the real world, Angel took a chance by leaving the military and then returning. I took a chance by moving to Washington, D.C. Life is full of chances. We discussed everything we did or thought about doing. She had my back and I had hers. We were locked in tight to support one another in whatever endeavor we were getting ready to embark on.

Life can be scary but sometimes the only thing holding you back is taking that chance, stepping out on faith, and praying that it will lead you in the right direction. As you take your chances, be sure to support and encourage your friends to do the same. And, when time permits, find something challenging to do together!

Key 24

FRIENDS THAT ARE
INVESTED IN THE FRIENDSHIP

"I learned that a real friendship is not about what you can get, but what you can give. Real friendship is about making sacrifices and investing in people to help them improve their lives."

Eric Thomas

I often come across people who do not know their best friends' parents. After Angel passed away, a few people asked if my parents knew her, and I was appalled at that question. It made me question what kind of best friends they had. In my mind, how can someone be your best friend and your parents don't know them? I knew her family and she knew my family, extended and immediate. Angel even attended a few family reunions with me. Whenever I mention my 'best friend' to anyone, family or friends, they know I am talking about Angel.

This entire book is about investing in your friendships, however, one of the biggest ways you can do this is by becoming involved in their life and allowing them to be involved in yours. Just as a potential spouse needs to meet your family and friends, your friends need to meet your family and other friends. A friend that is invested in meeting and knowing the people closest to you is the friend to have. They understand that knowing the family you were raised with can help them better understand who you are as a person and how you became the way you are. This makes the friendship extra special because you gain an understanding of each other you may not get on brunch or spa dates.

No matter the dynamics, family is important to us all. They are the first people we learn to interact with, they watch us grow and develop, and they know things about us that others may not be privy to. If you desire your friendship for the long haul, be sure to invest by allowing your friends to meet those that matter most to you.

"Anything is possible when you have the right people there to support you."

Misty Copeland

No one knows everything. Despite how wise, smart, and quick on our feet we may be in one area, we all have places in our lives where we are still learning how to navigate. For this reason, it's important for friends not to be harshly judgemental of each other. If your friendship is going to stand the test of time, you have to be okay with watching each other grow and mature. There will be seasons where you both make crazy decisions that you will later regret, however, the key is to be there to support each other through the consequences of those bad decisions. No one wants to hear, *"I told you so!"* Especially not when they are already ashamed of the decision they made. Friends should be loving, kind, and supportive of one another at all times, not just when it is easy.

Throughout the duration of our friendship, Angel and I made many mistakes in our personal lives. We have chosen the wrong path or done things that some people would frown upon. However, we never judged one another. I believe this is why we were safe spaces for each other. No matter how reckless or irresponsible I had been, I could tell Angel ANYTHING and she would talk it through with me. She never made me feel like I was a horrible person for making a wrong choice.

If there was something Angel wanted to do that I didn't agree with, I would tell her my opinion once and leave it at that. We would talk about the pros and cons, and she always knew I was there to support her no matter what her decision. If we had to pick up the pieces later it was never an *"I told you so"* that followed. Decisions were made before her death that her family and I will reap the consequences of for the rest of our lives, but I still don't feel like, *"I told you so!"* I know my friend made the best decisions she knew to make at the moment.

Life throws curve balls, and we never know how the tables will turn. We don't know today what we will learn tomorrow. Everyone can only do what they know to do today. When life brings the unexpected, it's more manageable when we know we have friends we can count on to hold our hand through the tears.

A Tribute to Our Angel

A FRIEND THAT WOULD RIDE HARDER FOR ME THAN I RODE FOR MYSELF

AMANDA FARRIOR

There was a time in my life when things were as upside down as the snow in a snow globe. After being in bed for days, ignoring calls, and completely detaching from life, Angel showed up at my house. She didn't care about the funk I was in or that I was disenchanted with life. She pulled up on me, didn't knock on the door, just came right in and encouraged me gently by saying, *"Bae, let's get up and go get a tattoo,"* with that beautiful smile on her face.

When I am in a mood, getting me out of the house isn't easy. However, Angel was also the one who would politely let you know she was not accepting *'no'* for an answer. Unbeknownst to Angel, I needed that *'hawk me down'* kind of love that day. On the way to the tattoo shop, she let me vent and cry and then told me, *"You are an amazing woman with a story to tell, we ain't gonna let life silence us."* That day she got a coy fish and I got an infinity symbol tattooed on my wrist.

I didn't want to push through my storm, but instead of judging, she encouraged me with such style and grace, the kind that only she could give. I was so thankful that she took time from her life to see me. But that's just who Angel was. When I wanted to give up, she would stand up and push me until I could push myself again.

"If not you, then who? If not now, then when?"

John F. Kennedy

Every day, life presents us with two paths. We can travel the road we always use, or we can choose the scenic route, filled with memories. We need friends who always seize the moment, and encourage us to do the same!

One thing Angel did was live! She always lived her life as if tomorrow wasn't promised. If she wanted to be a daredevil, she put on a harness and did it. If she wanted to try a new drink at a restaurant, she went in and bought it. She leaped over any obstacles between herself and any adventure she wanted. She would spend her last on anyone just so that they would have a good time.

One night in Las Vegas, we went in for the night, exhausted from the day. After being in the room for a little while, we decided we didn't want the night to end, so we headed out! We went down to the casino where the club was letting out to find some shenanigans to get into. I ran into a random man who gave me a $500 chip to gamble with. Angel and I used it as our opportunity to learn how to gamble. We did well and made our way up to $1500. I remember asking her if we should cash out or keep going.

We looked at each other and agreed to keep going! We thought we could bet big and win big, but ended up losing it all. We left with what we came with — nothing. However, everything we learned that night and the people we met made the shenanigans well worth it.

The next time a new opportunity lies in front of you and your bestie, seize the moment. Don't let it pass you by. Would you rather wonder how things could have gone, or reminisce on how things went? The choice is yours!

What About Your Friends?

Insert a picture of a time you
seized the moment with friends!

Key 27

FRIENDS THAT ACCEPT
YOU FOR WHO YOU ARE

"Everyone looks for different things in friendships, but deep down, everyone is trying to find the same stuff; acceptance and belonging."
Jessica Speer

Studies say that the best way to be successful in any relationship is to accept others for who they are. For some reason, when we connect with others, we analyze them in hopes that we can change them and make them more suitable for us. Naturally, we will see areas where others can improve, but in our friendships, it is vital to accept each other for who we are. If we are unable to accept each other, it will be difficult to appreciate what everyone brings to the friendship.

When it came to me, Angel accepted the good, bad, and the ugly. I wasn't judged for having an attitude one day or for doing the most at a party because I drank too much. As a friend, Angel never tried to turn me into something that I wasn't. If there was something I didn't want to do, she didn't make me do it. If there was something I didn't like, she didn't try to make me like it. The few things that we differed in still connected us because what she lacked, I could offer. And, whatever I lacked, she was always able to help me figure it out. She knew the real me, and never tried to change me one bit.

Accepting your friend as they are isn't about turning a blind eye to areas that need improvement. It's okay to give your friend advice and share wisdom when needed. However, your friendship shouldn't be built upon hopes that they will improve, but rather commitment to support them along the journey.

*"We'll be best friends forever because
you already know too much."*

Unknown

Growing up, I had some pretty unbelievable experiences. Many would probably hear my stories and think they were fabricated. Angel was the one person who could cosign on all of my stories because she was there in real-time or a part of my life when they happened. This picture was the beginning of a typical night out in DC, and it turned into a night filled with stories that I would give anything to hear her retell. The shenanigans that took place this night were unmatched. I am positive that everyone that was with us can recount how much fun we had and what a joy it was to be in Angel's presence. I recall telling stories to our friends about the things we did and the people we met, and Angel was always there to finish my story. Even when we talked if I mentioned something about a person she could already understand why I was bringing it up.

With true friends, there isn't a need for much background information to explain because they already know the context. They paid attention to the things you have told them in the past and when a topic is brought up, you can just jump right into the juicy details and waste no time catching everyone up to the story.

This is also where inside jokes are developed! You may see friends who just share a glance with one another and begin to laugh hysterically. This means they have shared enough moments together to have an infinite number of references and memories that can keep them laughing throughout the day. Measuring the amount of inside jokes you have with your friends will surely tell you just how close you are!

What About Your Friends?

Every friendship is filled with crazy stories and memories! Use the space below to write your favorite memory with friends. When you are done, give them a call to see how they remember the story!

_____

_____

_____

_____

_____

_____

_____

_____

_____

_____

_____

_____

"When the sun shines, we'll shine together.. Told you I'll be here forever.. Said I'll always be a friend... Took an oath I'ma stick it out 'til the end."

Umbrella, Rihanna

As far back as middle school, somehow I always chose friends who didn't feel the same about me as I felt about them. A few times, I ended up with a best friend who didn't consider me their best friend. It devastated me, and I vowed to never have a best friend again — until I met Angel. Although Angel and I were close, I don't think we actually referred to each other as best friends until about 3 or 4 years later. We had to be sure! She wanted to be my friend just as much as I wanted to be her friend. I understand now that our connection was divine and God-ordained, but of course, we didn't know that then.

One day, we were in church and someone told us that we were in each others' lives to intercede and be there for one another. God put us together to pray for one another, and we did. This is why our connection was deeper than friendship, we were connected in spirit.

You deserve friends who care as much about friendship as you do. You can always gauge a person's investment by watching their actions. If all else fails, get clarity on where you stand in each of your friends' lives. Don't be afraid to ask hard questions and be clear on what you mean to each other.

Key 30

FRIENDS THAT PRAY WITH YOU AND FOR YOU

"A true friend warms you with her presence, trusts you with her secrets, remembers you in her prayers."

It is cool to have friends to party with, but will those same friends say something to God about you? If the answer is no, then that is not a real friend. Everyone who knows Angel and I know we loved to have a good time. A best friend is someone who has a good time with you, BUT they are also someone who can pray with you. I prayed constantly for Angel, and she prayed for me as well. Many times, we would pray together over the phone.

When Angel struggled to make the weight requirement to get back into the military, she went home so her sister could help her train, eat right, and lose weight. One day, she called me super defeated. I was with my dad, so we stopped everything and my dad prayed with her. She felt so refreshed after that prayer. She had a new mojo to keep pressing, keep striving, and keep going. Angel eventually met her weight goal and was scheduled to go back into the military within a month!

Prayer changes things! When all seems lost, and you feel hopeless, praying brings you peace before your situation changes. Sometimes, along our life journey, there will be times when we don't have the strength to pray things through. That is why having friends who know how to play AND pray is vital. Having a friend who can pray for you and give you fresh new hope is beautiful. Just as much as you desire friends who will cover you in prayer, you must be a friend willing to cover your friends in prayer. Be intentional about helping your friends seek God for the wisdom, courage, faith, or discipline they need to move forward!

"Every minute spent in your company becomes the new greatest minute of my life."

Bolt

How do you feel when you see your friends? What is their reaction when you guys get together? No matter how long you have been friends, there should be excitement and joy when you see your friends. Very often, we find ourselves in a place where we just tolerate those in our lives. We no longer see how they fit in our lives, but we don't have the courage to say something or realign. Friends should not be people that you tolerate. You should find joy and happiness in the connection.

Whenever Angel and I saw each other, we were always thrilled to see one another. It didn't matter if we just saw each other that morning or had just gotten off the phone five minutes ago. From afar, one would think it had been years since we last encountered each other. We enjoyed each other's company that much.

I still remember the light that would beam in her eyes, and the smile she would have when we got together. It's a feeling that is hard to explain, a feeling of love directly from God. One day, Angel and an associate were at my house while I was at work. When I walked through the door, Angel jumped up to greet me, and the associate rolled their eyes, laughing at us. *"Y'all are obsessed with each other!"* They said as we chuckled. There was a slight mutual obsession and we loved it! It was nothing for Angel to say randomly, *"I love you, friend!"* And for me to reply, *"I love YOU, friend!"*

No matter how cheesy you may feel expressing your love and appreciation for your friendship, do it! You never know when you won't be able to tell them anymore. Even though losing Angel hurt tremendously, I have no regrets when it comes to her knowing how I felt about our friendship.

*"How lucky I am to have something
that makes saying goodbye so hard."*
Winnie the Pooh

Whenever I end a conversation or visit with one of my aunts, she never says goodbye. She says, *"Later!"* In fact, all of my mother's sisters say *"Later!"* before I end a call with them. I once thought it was an *'East St. Louis'* habit, but when I thought about it, *goodbye* sounds so permanent...even when we don't mean for it to be.

In this picture, Angel and I were together for my last night in Tampa before I moved to D.C. It was probably well past 4 am, but we didn't want to go to sleep. We knew once we woke up, I would be departing. So we challenged each other to stay up all night. There is a saying that goes, *"Goodbyes are not forever. They simply mean, 'I'll miss you until we meet again.'"* Every time Angel and I departed from each other, we hugged and said our goodbyes so formally that it was almost funny. We never wanted to see each other go, but we knew the next time we saw each other would be epic! Even when we were mad at each other, we still hugged it out upon our departure. We never took goodbye for granted.

I have been in relationships and friendships with people who would get angry and leave without saying goodbye. I am grateful Angel and I didn't exhibit that kind of behavior in our friendship. Anything can happen to us when we least expect it. Having friends that don't treat life casually or waste time on petty arguments is important. We need friends that still value the friendship when you are on bad terms. You may not want to hug each other but a simple text saying, *"I'll talk to you later,"* acknowledges that this is not the end and we will eventually work through it.

A Tribute to Our Angel

A FRIEND THAT WAS THERE FOR ME

TIA DEAS

I used to think friendships were overrated and didn't value the connections I had with the people. The broken home life I grew up in didn't aid the way I viewed relationships, but when Angel came into my life, things changed. I changed. She supported my

dreams. She supported my goals. She believed in me; more than I believed in myself. Angel was more than a friend and more than family to me. I can't quite think of a word to describe what she meant to me.

I cannot think of a better person to have had by my side to guide and help me become who I am today. With a smile or laugh, Angel was always there. I believe that was the best thing about her friendship. Happy or sad, in good graces or not, she always showed up or came through for me. I learned to be a friend because of her willingness to be a friend to me. Angel was an angel on Earth and I was one of many that were blessed to have her here.

FRIENDS THAT EMBRACE YOUR UNIQUENESS

"A great friendship is about two things: First, appreciating the similarities, and second, respecting the differences."

Unknown

Have you ever heard that opposites attract? Many people prefer to be around people who act, think, and operate just like them. However, there is so much beauty in having friends who are different from you or have different interests than you. No matter how similar you and a friend may seem, there are differences, and that's okay. The key is learning how to embrace those differences and appreciating what you both bring to the friendship.

Angel and I were a lot alike but there were a few areas where we differed. Angel liked basketball, I liked football. She played basketball while I was the cheerleader. She loved makeup and girly things while me, not so much. I was a little rough around the edges. If we were both at a party, I might end up being the center of attention while Angel enjoyed being in the background. I might end up engaging with 100 people while she stuck to her circle of friends.

At a family function, Angel knew I would introduce her to everyone in the room, which could be overwhelming in the grand scheme of things. At times, our differences could have become a burden on our friendship, but she accepted this about me. Even though it wasn't her thing, she enjoyed watching me mingle with other people. There was never any jealousy or animosity about me being a social butterfly. Angel used to say, *"Girl, you know a lot of people."* It was always a bonus because no matter where we traveled to or where we went, I always knew someone who was going to make sure we had a good time!

There are some character traits you will naturally adopt from your friends by spending time with them. However, there are certain things that are just unique about everyone. Don't take on the pressure of trying to become who your friends are, or make them like you. Challenge yourself to sit back, watch them in their element, and appreciate them for who they are. The best memories are made by individuals who are resolved to live and let others live!

FRIENDS THAT NURTURE YOU

"Friends are those rare people who ask how we are and then wait to hear the answer."

Ed Cunningham

One thing about me is that I am going to get sick, have an allergic reaction, or be overwhelmed with life at times. Angel always took care of me during those moments. She knew the foods I couldn't eat, the reactions they would cause, and where I kept my inhalers and EpiPens. She was naturally a nurturing person who would take care of you when you needed it. I went through three tragic losses while Angel was alive. I lost my godmother, then my paternal Grandfather and Aunt within a month of one another. No matter what Angel was going through at the time, she dropped everything and traveled to D.C. or Tampa to take care of me. There were many days when I couldn't get out the bed, and Angel cooked for me, washed my clothes, and cleaned my house. She took care of me like a mother would take care of her child.

Only a true friend will pick up your snotty tissues from crying all night and clean your dirty clothes as if it were normal. A person who would drop everything to be there for you in your time of need has a one-of-a-kind love for you. Many people are not in a position to drop everything and be there, no matter how good their intentions are. Sadly, I don't think I was in the position to return the favor or be that type of friend for Angel. She taught me not to do things with the hope of getting something in return. Angel did everything out of the kindness of her heart because that is who she was as a person.

As friends, we should do what we can to nurture each other. We may not always be able to be there at the drop of a dime, but we should be intentional about being there for our friends in their time of need. Sometimes, just sitting with them in silence is all they need to feel supported and loved. All relationships require nurturing, friendships are no exception. Nurture your friends and allow them to nurture you.

"It's an insane world but in it, there is one sanity; the loyalty of old friends."

Ben Hur

Everyone appreciated that Angel was a good listener. Angel listened intently to everything people shared with her, which made so many people feel like they had a deep connection with her. At times when we talked, she would get really silent. I would get irritated and change the subject, thinking she wasn't listening. She would go back to what I was saying and mention that she was thinking about what I had shared. She was actually digesting what I had to say. One day, I told her that I didn't feel as if I was as good of a listener as she was and she told me that was because I listened to respond and not to receive.

I had an issue that I talked with Angel about almost every day for at least three years. Each time, she listened diligently as I bickered, cried, and expressed my annoyance about the situation. She always acted as if it was her first time hearing it. It never annoyed her that I kept rehashing everything.

One day after she had been in the ER all day with her dad, he had recently had a heart attack, she texted me, "I know you are still hurting, but you have to pick up and move on from this situation, friend." She meant well and she was finally tired of hearing about it because of things going on in her personal life. Looking back, I can't believe I had the nerve to get mad. After she had listened to me for three years, she finally urged me to find a solution. I had to put my selfishness to the side and listen to her advice.

Learning how to be a good listener will take you far in life. It is a skill that makes you a better employee, business partner, spouse, and friend. It's hard to fight the urge to immediately give our thoughts. Some people do it because they want to instantly fix the issue being shared. We will find that sometimes, people can solve their own problems simply by hearing themselves talk about the situation. Every comment doesn't need a response or rebuttal. Sometimes, people just want to get things off their chest. A good friend knows when to comment and when to just be a listening ear.

My baby

"A true friend is someone who thinks that you are a good egg, even though he knows that you are slightly cracked."

Bernard Meltzer

Negative energy and people have a way of draining life out of every situation. Without a doubt, life gets hard, and there are moments when we can't see the silver lining in the dark clouds that surround us. This is why it is vital to surround ourselves with optimistic people who can pull us out of dark places and encourage us to keep looking forward.

Angel definitely had a "glass half full" mentality. You could never get her to think negatively about any situation. Part of this mentality was due to her strong faith in God. She always knew He would take care of her and bring her through any situation. At one point in Angel's life, she barely knew where her next meal was coming from but she would say, "I am not even worried. I have peace about it because I know God has me." I always loved that about her. At the beginning of our friendship, Angel didn't always see things with a positive perspective. My faith in God and the miracles she saw Him work in my life rubbed off on her. I always encouraged her to keep the faith and keep pressing through. In return, she did the same for me and others.

Having a positive attitude can improve even the worst situation. The ability to be optimistic is rooted in our faith in God. Knowing that He never turns a blind eye to our troubles encourages us to stay hopeful when our circumstances seem hopeless. Being optimistic isn't about ignoring the pain of your situation, but looking beyond the pain and having faith that God will turn your situation around. Strive to be a positive friend and make friends with positive people. Having positive people around us makes a large impact on our lives. I am grateful that Angel and I learned how to always see the glass half full. Our friendship was all the better because of our positive outlook on life.

"When good friends fight, it's not about who wins/loses, it's about who forgives, forgets, and still wants to be friends."

Unknown

I am not the easiest person to deal with. I often get in moods where I have a bad attitude or say things that are rude or insensitive. Despite all of this, Angel forgave me. Our disagreements and arguments were always short-lived because we understood that the good in our relationship will always outweigh the bad. Some things were not even worth being mad about for more than ten minutes over. Even if we wanted to hate each other, we couldn't because we had too much fun around each other. If we didn't verbally forgive each other, we recognized that we would lose more than a friendship if we didn't forgive. We would lose an irreplaceable lifetime bond, so it was important to work through any issue we had.

We all make mistakes, and misjudgments, and do things that hurt others, even when we don't try. It is important to forgive often and fast. Also, it's important to remember that even though we meet each other one way, we grow and change. In order to do life with friends, you must be able to forgive and give grace for everyone to grow and mature.

What About Your Friends?

Insert pictures of friends you know will remain your friend, no matter what!

FRIENDS WITH SIMILAR
VALUES AND MORALS

*"One of the most beautiful qualities
of true friendship is to understand
and to be understood."*

Seneca

When you have a friend that shares common goals with you it is easy to uplift and support one another. More important than having similar goals is having similar mindsets. Being of like mind means you agree on morals, values, and perspectives on life. You may have a different way of acting out those things, but at the core of the matter, you think the same.

Personally, Angel wanted to be a wife, have a family, and have a white picket fence, and so did I. Naturally, she encouraged me to pursue the life that would make my goals of being a wife and having kids a reality. Professionally, Angel and I wanted to be successful in our careers. Her goal was to become a Non-Commissioned Officer in the Army and my goal was to become a Senior Executive in the government. Our career paths just so happen to run concurrently with one another, but the main goal was to make it to the top ranks. It wasn't good enough to just be in the military, she wanted to be an officer. For me, it wasn't good enough to just have a government position, I wanted to be a senior executive. She was able to assist in organizing resumes and I was good at writing letters of recommendation or being a reference point of contact. If I needed help or she needed assistance, we were always there to utilize each others' strengths because we both strived for higher positions within our careers. We encouraged one another and helped each other set goals that we knew we could reach.

When you have like-minded friends, it's easier to hold each other accountable and push each other toward success. On the other hand, if you don't have friends who are like-minded, your focus and drive can come off as extra or unnecessary. Everyone wants what they want in life. Additionally, we all see the world according to our experiences. Rather than force people to get on the same page as you, find friends who have similar morals and values.

FRIENDS YOU CAN TALK TO ABOUT ANYTHING

"It's the friends you can call up at 4 a.m. that matter."

Marlene Dietrich

A true friend will not pick and choose which conversations you share. Some conversations will be exciting and some may be saddening, however, your bestie will be willing to discuss it all. Angel and I talked about everything from work, to relationships, to marriage, to death. Ironically, we talked about death a lot, even leading up to her last days. We would often joke about people who would act out if we died or how we would react at each others' funerals, oblivious that that reality was around the corner.

I remember how eager she was to see me before she got deployed. I think that she thought something was going to happen to her overseas when she deployed with the military the following month. Although she was excited because I told her about my experiences in the country she was deploying to, I think she still had a lot of anxiety about it. I was also nervous about her going over there, but I didn't want to stress her out. We didn't dwell on the elephant in the room that both of us were experiencing.

In the week leading up to her last days, I told her that I felt as though I was getting ready to tragically lose someone close to me. It had been heavy in my spirit all week. I prayed about it, asked God to prepare me for what was to come, and I talked to Angel about it. I recall being near tears telling her about this awful feeling. She told me, *"You know when you get that feeling, you are never wrong."* I had felt the same before my grandfather passed.

As we talked that evening, her words to me were very comforting. She told me that even though it had been years since her grandmother passed, she still grieved her heavily. Remembering the good times, how she made her feel, and that she was in a better place helped her get through when the grief was too heavy to bear.

Angel shared that with me just four days before she was brutally murdered. I can still hear her words in the back of my mind. Immediately after she passed, I remembered our conversation. I had Angel's comforting words to carry me through that fateful weekend.

If your friend seems pressed about something, be attentive and give a listening ear. It may not make much sense to you at the moment, but you never know what could be around the corner. Our friends should feel safe discussing any topic with us. Likewise, we should have friends who don't make us feel strange, whether we are talking about a new love interest or fear about the future. All conversations should be welcomed in healthy, genuine friendships.

"True friends are always together in spirit."

Anne, *Anne of Green Gables*

When you share a deep connection with someone, sometimes you don't have to talk to them to understand how they are feeling or what they need. When you have spent time understanding your friends' personalities, habits, and quirks, you develop a deeper bond and can be what they need.

Your best friend may not be much of a phone person, but that doesn't make them any less of a friend because you talk to them once a week versus every day. Every friendship is different. There were times when Angel just wanted to listen to her music, and I just wanted to read a book. We didn't have to fill every minute of our time together with something extravagant. Sometimes, life got crazy and just being in each others' presence was enough.

Because we understood our connection, it wasn't hard to pick up on what we needed at the moment. Even when Angel was miles away sometimes, I could just feel that she was not having a good day. I would text her a song and she would say *thanks I really needed that.* Many times I could feel her thinking about me and vice versa. I would be thinking about her or talking about her to someone, and she would call and say, *"I felt you thinking about me!"* It was very weird, almost like we were twins.

Our connection was so deep that when she went into labor I had stomach pains as if I felt her contractions. After she was murdered, I had a very empty feeling in my soul because I could no longer feel her moods or sense her thinking about me. I know our connection was divine. It was beautiful, a connection that some people may never get to experience. If you are ever blessed with this kind of relationship with a spouse, friend, or family member, cherish it. Those relationships are truly blessed by God.

Key 41

FRIENDS THAT YOU KNOW
YOU WILL SEE AGAIN

"Can miles truly separate you from friends? If you want to be with someone you love, aren't you already there?"

Richard Bach

The last time I physically saw Angel was a chilly morning in February. She was leaving my house that morning to be sworn into the military again. She had about a three-hour drive from my house in Washington, DC to Norfolk, VA. We said our goodbyes that morning, I got in my car and left for work, and she sat in her parked car, waiting for it to warm. I was late to work, per usual, and as I sped away, she called me and said she forgot to give me my key. When I pulled up to her car, I expected to just grab the key and speed back off to work since we had already said our goodbyes. Instead, she got out of her car, I followed suit, and we hugged each other for a long time. She had tears in her eyes and being my usual insensitive self I asked, *"Girl, what's wrong with you?"*

"I am just really going to miss you!" she said through her tears. *"Aww friend, I am going to miss you too! But we have been praying for this and now it's finally time!"* I encouraged her. She walked back to her car, we looked at each other again, and I was like, *"Give me one more hug, girl!"* We were always a little over

dramatic when we said our goodbyes, but that time felt a little different. It was almost as if we knew that would be our last time together. Our last time embracing each other was very surreal.

"To be absent from the body, is to be present with the Lord."
2 Corinthians 5:8

Both people in this photo made a great impact on who I am today, and both are no longer here. Demerrio Tobler was an awesome prayer warrior and worship leader who hilariously made sure I stayed on the straight and narrow while I was in college. I remember this night he saw us out the door on the way to the homecoming dance and took pictures with us. He knew Angel and I were about to be in some shenanigans and he probably wouldn't see us again once the party started. Sadly, he was killed a few years later (2017) by a drunk driver in a head-on car collision. His death was one of the first times I really tried to understand and grasp the concept that I need to see my friends again on the other side.

Recently, I was looking at a picture of Angel and I that I posted in 2011. The caption I wrote under it said, *"Those who live in the Lord will see each other again."* Immediately after Angel passed away, I had a weird peace because I knew in my heart that she was okay. I knew that she was saved, had asked Jesus to forgive her, and that God gave her time to get whatever she needed to get right to have eternal life. My spirit was well with that. Despite literally EVERYTHING that went on with the way she passed away and the drama involved, I knew that she received her crown. Knowing that I will see her again brings me much comfort through my time of grief.

FRIENDS THAT ALIGN
WITH YOUR PURPOSE

*"The most beautiful discovery true
friends make is that they can grow
separately without growing apart."*
Elisabeth Foley

P rayer shaped our adult lives and God ordered our steps right
until the very end of Angel's life. There were many times
Angel was struggling, and we would pray about it. Afterward,
she would be at such peace about whatever situation was going
on. I read a book called *The 40-Day Prayer Challenge* by Mark
Batterson and I told Angel how this book changed my life. She
suggested we start a book club and invite other people to read it
with us.

Every day, we read a passage and discussed what we thought
about the reading for the day. The insight Angel gathered from the
book was so touching to me, and I definitely saw her prayer life
strengthen

We finished the book, and Angel went home for the holidays.
This was a couple of weeks before she passed away. She visited our
childhood church and called me after service to share how good
she felt and how everyone showed her so much love. She sounded
so happy. I could hear and see the joy of the Lord in her heart and
all over. I know for a fact God was ordering her steps. That book

helped her reach her purpose and get her life together before she passed away.

That final trip she took back home was nothing short of perfect for her and everyone who saw her. It saddens me deeply that I couldn't join her on that trip but looking back, everyone she spent time with during that trip needed that last time to feel her love.

Not only did I help Angel in her purpose, but she helped me in mine. After she passed away I started a book club because she encouraged me to. I started a YouTube channel because she encouraged me to. I am writing a book as she encouraged me to. I am telling my story like she always told me to. And, I am going to be someone great because she always told me I would be. I truly didn't start walking in my purpose until after Angel passed away.

I always knew that she would be an important motivating factor for me to be successful, but I never knew it would be because of her. She would always tell me that I would touch many lives, and I would always say, *"Yup, and you are going to be right there with me while I'm doing it!"* She's not here physically but she is here with me spiritually because she gave me the extra boost to do what God called me to do.

Because of circumstances I went through growing up, I always knew my calling was to battered women. When Angel was brutally murdered in a domestic violence incident, I felt more inclined to help and be a resource for anyone who wants to receive help.

The purpose alignment between Angel and I is very rare. Your best friend might not be directly aligned with your purpose, but you can still choose a best friend that will support you as you operate in your purpose.

Reflections

Use the following pages to reflect on your friendships and the role you play as a friend. Allow the prompts to guide you as you consider the health of your friendships!

Let's Talk About Your Friends!

Share keys that you recognize in your friends.

_____

_____

_____

_____

_____

_____

_____

_____

_____

_____

_____

_____

_____

_____

_____

_____

_____

_____

_____

_____

Which keys do you think are your strengths as a friend?

_____

_____

_____

_____

_____

_____

_____

_____

_____

_____

_____

_____

_____

_____

_____

_____

_____

_____

_____

_____

_____

Which keys do you need to improve in to be a better friend?

_____

_____

_____

_____

_____

_____

_____

_____

_____

_____

_____

_____

_____

_____

_____

_____

_____

_____

_____

_____

_____

_____

Which keys do you look for when making new friends?

_____

_____

_____

_____

_____

_____

_____

_____

_____

_____

_____

_____

_____

_____

_____

_____

_____

_____

_____

_____

_____

What is the most rewarding part about being a good friend?

_____

_____

_____

_____

_____

_____

_____

_____

_____

_____

_____

_____

_____

_____

_____

_____

_____

_____

_____

_____

_____

_____

What is most rewarding part of having good friends?

_____

_____

_____

_____

_____

_____

_____

_____

_____

_____

_____

_____

_____

_____

_____

_____

_____

_____

_____

_____

_____

_____

Dear Best Friend,

Letter writing is such a lost art. In a world filled with social media, text messages, and emails, it warms my heart to get a letter or a card from someone expressing themselves. As you were reading this book, I'm sure a few friends came to mind. Take out a sheet of paper and write a letter to a friend about the keys you appreciate in your friendship. A few words from the heart can go a long way!

What About Your Friends?

Insert pictures of friends you really miss!

Our Dear Angel,

Our hands can no longer embrace you. Our eyes can no longer behold you. It will be awhile before we can share a laugh with you. However, our hearts will never forget how you made us feel. We love you, and we miss you.

Your Loving Family

Angel
and
Loved Ones

My Ride or Die

TIKIRA KNOWLES

Angel was the friend I could call on no matter the circumstances, how high the stakes, or how bad the consequences. She was always reliable and dependable. She was inspiring. Without trying, she pushed me to be the best version of myself. Angel encouraged me to continue to seek positive change and growth. She taught me how to inspire others. The high regard that she held for me fueled my motivation to live and lead by example. I am forever grateful for the mark Angel left on my life. I was privileged to share such a close bond with her. Love, loyalty, transparency, and genuine support is hard to come by. I received all of that from my "ride or die."

My Angel From Above

BRISHAUNA CONNER

Although I only knew Angel for a short amount of time, it felt like I had known her my whole life. When I first met Angel back in 2019, I was so excited to meet her. We would always talk about her son, Stephon, and her love for beauty care such as hair, lashes, and makeup. Angel was the first person to reach out to me from my dad's side of the family. Until her, I had never met anyone from my paternal side of the family. She took the time to introduce me to other family members and ensured people in the family knew who I was.

When I finally met Angel in person, I felt like the other half of me was complete. Angel took me in as if I was her little sister. I remember the first time we met in person to have lunch, we made plans to travel to different places with the rest of our family. Angel was the big sister I always wanted. Losing her changed everything. She inspired me in so many ways. It is my goal to help continue her legacy as much as possible.

My Light-Skinned Twin

CHARLIE PULLUM
Her Chocolate Twin

Angel's boldness and personality preceded her. When you met her, you already knew she was THAT CHICK. She possessed so much wisdom and empowerment. We often shared thoughts with one another or she would call me for advice. Angel was more than my baby cousin. She was like a daughter to me. Her mother, my Aunt Gail, would often tell me how she reminded her of me. At first, I didn't see it. However, as she got older, there was no denying it. Even when her son, Stephon, made his debut on earth, he looked just like my son, Major. Angel often told me that she looked up to me as a role model.

Those words will forever be etched in my heart. Angel and I would have so many beautiful memories together. We often vacationed in Miami on Memorial Day weekend, and we always had a good time. I'll never forget how we were able to hold each other up by being STRONG BLACK WOMEN. Though she is no longer with us, I have a hanging plant over my bed that I named "Angel." I know she keeps watch over me. This paragraph was by far the HARDEST thing I've ever had to write. I miss her everyday, but my comfort is in knowing she is resting in God's arms.

There Are No Words

JESSICA CONNER
Her Sister

Angel was the best sister I could have ever imagined having. I miss her so much. I am so proud of the woman she became and the legacy she left. Angel, no matter what, I got your back. I have Stephon's back too. You're my bighead always. I love you. RAWR

My Sweet Angel La'Vine

GAIL CONNER
Her Loving Mother

Angel was born premature. I had so many problems carrying her that I thought we would lose her…BUT GOD. This is one of the reasons her father, Jeff, and I named her Angel La'Vine. Angel was the cutest baby. She had big brown eyes and would just stare at you and watch your every move. Her gaze was so strong that some people thought she was a baby doll. She was a very quiet baby, even shy. As we continued to raise her, we saw

that she had a good and loving heart. I watched Angel slowly grow into her name. People made fun of her for having big eyes, so I told her the next time someone teased her eyes reply, *"BUT THEY'RE PRETTY!"* I overheard her tell a child that one day and I smiled on the inside because she was gaining the confidence that I taught her to have. Her confidence definitely blossomed, and she made many friends and acquaintances from the neighborhood to around the world after she enlisted into the Army. I never realized just how many people Angel impacted until she was gone. People loved my daughter. I was thankful that no matter where she was stationed, she always made friends. I missed her while she was away in the military, but she gave me the best gift I could ever receive, her son,

Stephon. When Angel told us she was pregnant, we were so happy. My heart overflowed with love for him before I even saw his little face. I am very proud that God chose me to be his "Nana." Angel soon got out of the military to be closer to home to assist her father and I as we dealt with various medical issues. As a single mother, Angel needed help raising her son. For his first seven years of life, he lived under our roof while Angel served in the Army Reserves and

worked multiple jobs to provide a better life for Stephon. Then, January 18, 2020 our Angel was gone. It was one of the worst days of our lives. Just when we thought it couldn't get any worse, a few months later, our grandson was gone too. Although he was ordered to go live with his father, it was like a second death or trauma that we had to deal with in a short time. Up until Stephon left us, Jeff was the only father he knew. They were inseparable, and had a bond similar to the one Angel and Jeff shared.

Angel and her father shared the same zodiac sign and would often say this is what brought them close. Every year, Angel would take him to a pro football game. It was one of their bonding moments and Jeff looked forward to it every year. For Jeff, losing Angel, his baby girl was detrimental. After losing a twin brother at a young age, a son in 2007, and having a son incarcerated for over 30 years, losing another loved one was unimaginable for Jeff. Traveling to Oklahoma for court dates and to North Carolina for custody hearings and visitation rights took a toll on Jeff and his health. In April 2022, we finally got a guilty verdict for the person who murdered our Angel. He was sentenced to life in prison without the possibility of parole. Shortly after that, on June 28, 2022, Angel's 31st birthday, Jeff passed away. The pain of missing his daughter finally took a toll on him and he was able to wish Angel a Happy Birthday himself.

After her passing away, Jeff and I realized the impact that Angel had in many people's lives. Angel's lifetime of being a good friend to others came back to us in ways we never imagined. Her friends comforted us in the loss of our grandchild and dealing with the loss of Angel as well. Angel's friends are always there to talk to me on the phone, help me look up laws that can help me retain visitation with my

grandson, speak on behalf of Angel and the family in relation to gun violence and domestic abuse, and so much more. These are all very important reminders to me of the type of friend that Angel was. Her friends provided my family and I with so much love and

support. Angel's friendship is a large part of her legacy.

Angel,

Even though your heart is resting, I still have five heartbeats: your son, Stephon, your sister, Jessica, your brothers, Pookey & Aaron, & your Aunt Jackie. Your heart will continue to beat with us.

Love Mom,
Patricia Gail Conner

Acknowledgements

I would like to thank the Conner Family for allowing me to be there for them during the extremely difficult process of grieving and healing. You didn't have to include my family and I, but you did, and it means the world to me. Special thanks to Jessica Conner for sharing her sister with me and allowing me to express my grief in my own way. You were Angel's first best friend, and the things you taught her through being her big sister are what made her the bestest friend I could have ever had. I love you forever, Big Sister! To the extended family, thank you for your support in finishing this book. The Conner Family will always have a daughter/sister/niece/cousin in me.

I also want to thank my family. It's been a challenging journey for us as well. To my mom, Yvette Torbert, thank you for listening to the tears, silent and loud. To my dad, Shelton Torbert, thank you for holding me accountable during my depression, dropping everything when I needed to get home, to include traveling 100 miles away going 5mph in a snowstorm to rescue me because depression got the best of me. That was a scary seven hour trip that only God brought us through. To my brothers, Marcus and Shelton Torbert Jr., thank you both for constantly checking on me night and day.

Mother Brenda Tolson, thank you for reminding me to finish the book when I swept it under the rug. I am additionally grateful for the many, many people who have been praying for me from the beginning of the tragedy until now. To my friend group in DC who were at my house to greet me as soon as I landed after the tragedy (Jennifer, Kristi, Casey, Zaneta, T-Y, Nigel), thank you. You were very instrumental to my healing process. To my First Baptist Church of Glenarden family, my Queen Esther Sisters (Deborah, Kiara, Camille, Keiana) who decorated my place to bring me comfort and love during my bereavement, my college and childhood friends and family who sent gifts remembering Angel (Kade, Keyonna, Lisa, Belinda), thank you. Thank you to Faith, Dejah, Hans, Shara, Paris, Elizabeth, the DeSaussure Family, Moore Family, and the Shiloh Christian Family for their support and assistance in the homegoing services for Angel. The outpouring of love was tremendous. I felt every prayer, and they helped me to get up every day when I didn't want too. Those prayers helped me through the days when I couldn't pray for myself. Those prayers kept me in my right mind when the devil worked through numerous other avenues to destroy me while I was grieving.

I would also like to thank KVP (Keen Vision Publishing) for taking on my project, guiding me every step of the way, taking care of the project as if they knew Angel personally, and helping my vison come to life. Even when I got hard to deal with, they remained professional. I just had to keep in mind that everything happens in God's timing. I am happy we didn't rush this project because now, it is exactly how God intended for it to be!

I appreciate Rev. Kerry Warner for the suggestion and direction. Thank you to my Aunt Wanda Moore & Triona Roberts for writing books for their lost loved ones and inspiring me to do the same. Aniyah Watkins, you are my blessing in disguise. To everyone who has supported me on this journey and followed Angel's story, THANK YOU! I pray that God will bless all of you as He has blessed me!

About The Author

Shalicia LaShaye Torbert currently resides in Washington DC, working as a Budget & Programming Analyst for the Department of Defense (DoD). Having over 11 years of multi-faceted experience in the DoD and traveling to numerous countries to get the job done, in 2017 she was awarded The Joint Civilian Service Commendation Award, a prestigious military award for the extensive work she performed overseas in support of the Nation. She holds a Masters in Business Administration from Troy University,

where she also studied for her Masters in International Relations minoring in National Security. She graduated from the University of South Florida with an undergraduate degree in Finance. While attending the University of South Florida she was honored as one of the top 25 students under 25 in the College of Business c/o 2013. In 2020, she graduated with certificates from the University of Alabama at Birmingham where she studied Non-Profit Management & Social Media Analysis. Shalicia also is the founder of Queendom Business, a nonprofit initiative to help people navigate through painful or traumatic life experiences and turn them into something positive. She loves doing outreach through hosting events and getting involved in her community.

She also has a monthly podcast on her Instagram and YouTube channels called Transformation Tuesdays where she discusses different hot topics. Also, she hosts the Queendom Business Book Club, a Co-Ed book club that reads a different book every month. In 2023, based on her academic achievements and community involvement, she was awarded honorary membership in Zeta Omicron Chapter of Iota Phi Lambda Sorority, Incorporated, the first African American greek-lettered business sorority. In her spare time, she serves as the secretary on her neighborhoods Homeowners Association Board, being a public notary, volunteering in the college ministry at her church, and representing up and coming musical artists as a talent manager and executive producer. She also participates in mentoring students at Ohio State University through the Undergraduate Society of Black Leaders.

Connect with the Author

Thank you for supporting and reading, *Lessons From An Angel*. The author would love to connect with you! Here are a few ways you can connect with Shalicia, stay updated on events, and receive information about the amazing things in store for this project and future projects. Feel free to tag us on Instagram with pictures and use the hashtag #LessonsFromAnAngel.

EMAIL   shayetorbert@gmail.com
INSTAGRAM   @LessonFromAnAngel
YOUTUBE   Shaye Torbert - @QueendomBusiness

If you or a family member is experiencing any type of domestic violence or feel you are in danger, call the National Domestic Violence Hotline at 1.800.799.SAFE (7233) or text "START" to 88788, they will provide you with 24/7 access to resources and support.

Your life matters.